P9-CJZ-903

FIRST AMERICANS
The Hopi

RUTH BJORKLUND

Marshall Cavendish
Benchmark
New York

ACKNOWLEDGMENTS

Series consultant: Raymond Bial

Marshall Cavendish
99 White Plains Road
Tarrytown, New York 10591-5502
www.marshallcavendish.us

Text, maps, and illustrations copyright © 2009 by Marshall Cavendish Corporation
Map and craft illustrations by Chris Santoro

Library of Congress Cataloging-in-Publication Data
Bjorklund, Ruth.
The Hopi / by Ruth Bjorklund.
p. cm. — (First Americans)
Summary: "Provides comprehensive information on the background, lifestyle, beliefs, and present-day lives of the Hopi people"
—Provided by publisher.
Includes bibliographical references and index.
ISBN 978-0-7614-3021-6
1. Hopi Indians—History—Juvenile literature.   2. Hopi Indians—Social life and customs—Juvenile literature.   I. Title.
E99.H7B56 2009
979.1004'97458—dc22
2007033676

Front cover: A Hopi girl attends the famous Indian Crafts Fair, Santa Fe, New Mexico.
Title page: Detail of a beautifully woven garment worn at Hopi ceremonies
Photo research by: Connie Gardner
Cover photo by Robert Frerck/Odyssey Productions
The photographs in this book are used by permission and through the courtesy of:
Corbis: Bob Rowan, title page, 27, 36; Macduff Everton, 6; CORBIS, 12,17; Tom Bean, 14, 39; Gunter Marx, 16; Buddy Mays, 20; Michael T. Sedara, 24; Catherine Karnow, 31; Geoffrey Clements, 33; Stephen Mopope, 34; George H.H. Huey, 38; *Getty Images:* Tom Till, 5; Hulton Archive, 7, 9, 23; *Art Resource:* Smithsonian American Art Museum, Washington, DC, 18; Werner Forman, 30; *Nativestock:* Marilyn "Angel" Wynn, 21, 39.

Editor: Deborah Grahame
Publisher: Michelle Bisson
Art Director: Anahid Hamparian
Series Designer: Symon Chow

Printed in Malaysia
1 3 5 6 4 2

CONTENTS

1 · PEACEFUL, GOOD, AND WISE

More than ten thousand years ago, the ancestors of the Hopi tribe moved north from what is now Mexico. They settled in the region called the Four Corners, the area in the United States where four states touch—Colorado, Utah, Arizona, and New Mexico. They were hunters and gatherers who followed herds of mammoth and bison and collected wild berries, grasses, and nuts. For shelter they built pit-houses underground. Later these people, whom the Hopi call the Ancient Ones, built large mud and stone villages high on cliffs overlooking what is today called the Grand Canyon. The Ancient Ones were clever. They farmed, hunted, made tools and pottery, and traded widely with other villages. Their cities were some of the grandest on the continent. But in the

The Ancient Ones built cliff dwellings such as this one which has more than one hundred rooms.

Storm clouds gather over Black Mesa.

1200s CE, the region's climate turned hot and dry, and the Ancient Ones mysteriously left, leaving their cities behind.

Around the time of this big change, small groups of Hopi settled in valleys near a high, flat-topped mountain called Black **Mesa**. The area was dry and rugged, but there was enough water and protection from the strong winds for the Hopi to set up permanent villages. Here the Hopi learned new ways to plant corn, squash, and other crops that could grow in dry soil. They hunted small animals, gathered wild plants, and lived peacefully among themselves and other desert tribes. Then, in the 1500s, **hostile** raiding tribes from the north and powerful Spanish explorers from the south moved into Hopi territory.

In 1540 Francisco Vásquez de Coronado led an army of soldiers from Mexico in search of gold. He set up a camp near

Spanish soldiers entered Hopi lands and built a mission on each mesa.

a Hopi village. The Hopi did not want to share their land with the newcomers at first. After a while the Hopi acted as wilderness guides and shared food and other supplies. The explorers called the Hopi and other village tribes the Pueblo Indians. *Pueblo* is Spanish for "village." The Spanish believed the area was rich with gold and tried to claim treasures for their king. While exploring the area they made many brutal demands on the Pueblo people. In 1598 one explorer, Don Juan de Oñate, claimed Hopi lands for Spain. Years later Spanish priests set up churches and missions to try to make the Pueblo people give up their native religion and accept the **Catholic** faith. The priests forced the Pueblo Indians to work their farms and tend their livestock. Their cruelty angered the Pueblo people, who secretly planned a revolt. In 1680 the Hopi, along with other Pueblo tribes, overthrew the Spanish. After the Pueblo Revolt, the Hopi lived in peace for twelve years. They returned to farming, hunting, and practicing their own religion. But they had also learned from the Spanish how to raise sheep, cattle, horses, and burros. They grew new crops such as peaches, melons, apples, chili peppers, and tomatoes, and began to use metal tools such as knives, saws, scissors, and nails.

Hopi herders watch over their sheep and goats.

In 1692 the Spanish returned. The Hopi moved from their valleys to the top of Black Mesa. They formed villages on three mesas, which they named First Mesa, Second Mesa, and Third Mesa. From these high points they could see their enemies coming. The three mesas allowed the Hopi to live peacefully for many decades. But the world changed around them. The Navajo moved closer to Hopi territory, grazed their livestock on Hopi land, and raided Hopi

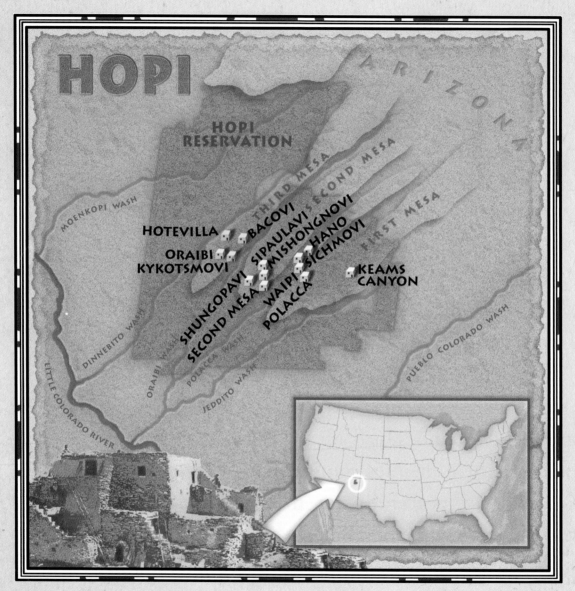

This map of Hopi lands shows First Mesa, Second Mesa, and Third Mesa as they reach out from Black Mesa like fingers.

villages. In 1821 Mexico gained independence from Spain, and Hopi land became a part of Mexico. Hopi people were declared Mexican citizens. But in 1848 Mexico lost to the United States in the Mexican-American War. The ancestral land of the Hopi became a part of the United States. The United States did not grant citizenship to Indian people, including the Hopi, until 1924.

Americans continued to travel and trade in Hopi territory. The U.S. Army built a fort called Fort Defiance on Hopi land to protect Americans from the attacks of hostile tribes. Railroads were built across the country, making it easier for American settlers to form new towns. The Hopi worried about the newcomers using up precious water. They spoke with agents of the American government. In 1882 President Chester A. Arthur signed an order that created a **reservation** for the Hopi. The Hopi wanted the reservation to protect them, but in the late 1880s the American government built a school on the reservation and forced Hopi children to attend.

A Hopi man sits at home beside two Hopi girls doing chores.

Many Hopi parents kept their children home, afraid that the school would destroy their traditional way of life. American government agents punished them, sending some fathers to prison. They also demanded that Hopi men and boys cut their long hair short and stop their religious ceremonies. They wanted the Hopi to look like European-Americans, speak only English, and practice the Christian religion.

In 1934 the Hopi people created a Tribal Council so that they could speak to the U.S. government with one voice. The Hopi also developed a constitution that gave them laws to follow as an independent nation within the United States. But not until 1948 did the state of Arizona allow the Hopi and other tribes to vote in state and federal elections.

The Hopi have lived in the same villages for a long time, and have held on to their traditions. They practice their own religion, speak their own language, and keep many ceremonies secret from outsiders. The Hopi stay true to their name and their belief in what they call the "Hopi Way." *Hopi* is short for *Hopituh Shi-nu-mu*, which means "people who are peaceful, good, and wise."

2 · THE THREE MESAS

Although the region where they live is dry, rocky, windy, and sometimes very harsh, the Hopi have stayed in the same villages and farmed the same land longer than any other Native American people anywhere in North America. Each Hopi family group, or **clan**, has a home in a village on one of the three mesas, farmlands in the valley, and hunting grounds beyond.

Long ago, family groups lived together in houses made of sandstone and dried mud, or **adobe**. The buildings were close to each other, like apartment buildings. Inside, there were separate areas for keeping **sacred** objects, storing food, cooking, eating, sleeping, and family activities. The houses were two or three floors high. People climbed ladders to get to each level. During hot summers, many climbed to their rooftops

Traditional Hopi hunting grounds surround Black Mesa.

Many Hopi dwellings were multilevel and housed more than one generation.

and slept under the stars. Hopi houses lined streets that led to a central plaza used for public gatherings. Near each plaza was a **kiva**, a special underground room where men's religious meetings were held. Every morning from the central plaza, a man known as the town crier, or crier chief, shouted out the news of the day and told everyone when it was time to go to work.

Hopi men and women had different but equally important duties. The men were skillful farmers who built systems to catch rainwater and ditches to carry water to their fields. They planted and harvested crops such as corn, beans, squash, melons, and cotton. After harvesting cotton, the men wove it into cloth to make robes, shirts, aprons, and wide shawl-like dresses called **mantas**. They

A Hopi girl wears the special manta shawl and other traditional clothing.

In this painting, a Hopi man weaves a rug using a bold geometric pattern.

also wove special sashes for their brides to wear on their wedding day. Hopi men hunted rabbits and small game and deer and bison, and raised wild turkeys to eat. To catch small game, they built walls of netting and chased rabbits and squirrels toward the nets. They captured the animals by throwing long wooden sticks at them. When necessary, the men formed hunting parties to hunt deer, antelope, and bison. They chased the animals into **box canyons** and shot them with bows and arrows. Besides bringing meat back to the village, the men used the bones and the **sinews** of the animals to make bows and arrows, sewing needles, and other useful tools. They also used the skins of the animals for making drums, leggings, and moccasins. Hopi men raised sheep and sheared the wool to make blankets, warm winter clothing, and rugs. Near Black Mesa, they discovered coal in the mountains and mined it to use as fuel for cooking, firing pottery, and heating. They also dug colored stones—especially **turquoise**—and traded for coral shells to make jewelry. Both men and women wore

These modern pieces of jewelry are made of silver and turquoise and show traditional Hopi designs such as rain clouds and cornstalks.

bracelets, necklaces, and decorative beads on their clothing.

Women owned the houses and the family lands. When men married they moved to the home of their wife's mother. Large families made up of grandparents, parents, aunts and uncles, children, and cousins were part of a group called a clan. Hopi clans were related through mothers. Women managed the homes and land and were the heads of families

Piki

Every day, Hopi women made a thin bread called **piki**. The bread was cooked on hot stones, but today many Hopi cook it with a flat pan. You will be working by a hot stove, so be sure that an adult is nearby to help you. You will need:

- Measuring cups
- Wooden spoon
- A pan or griddle
- Spatula
- Mixing bowl
- Serving plate
- Cooking oil
- 2 cups blue cornmeal
- $1\frac{1}{4}$ cups water

A girl mixes blue corn and water to make her family's daily serving of piki bread.

Wash your hands. Measure the cornmeal and water and place in the mixing bowl. Stir with the wooden spoon, or your hands, until the dough is moist and feels like elastic. You do not want the dough to be sticky. Divide the dough into 12 equal pieces. Form 12 dough balls. Flatten each ball until it is thin and round. Place the pan or griddle on the stove and turn the temperature to medium heat. Pour a few drops of cooking oil into the pan. Once the pan or griddle has heated up, place one of the piki on it. Cook until golden brown. With the spatula, flip the piki and cook briefly on the other side. Remove and place the piki on a plate. Repeat until all of the piki are cooked. Enjoy with beans, soup, or a bit of sugar.

and clans. Among their many duties, women cleaned, prepared food, and took care of children and the home. They knew which berries and wild plants, such as **piñon** nuts, to gather and eat. They also collected the **yucca** cactus from which they made food and drink as well as soap, hairbrushes, serving trays, and baskets. Every day women and girls ground corn into meal. Besides making food and baskets in which to store the food, women also made pottery from clay. They used their pots to store and cook food and to carry water from the springs. Pots and baskets were decorated with traditional Hopi symbols such as snakes, eagles, bears, rainbows, rain, clouds, and lightning bolts.

When children were born, it was a cause for great celebration. A baby spent the first nineteen days of life alone with its mother before being brought out into the sunshine to greet the world and the rest of the clan. On that twentieth day, the child was given a special blanket, a perfect ear of corn, and a name. Children's names came from nature, such as Snake Girl, Water Moon, Strong Deer, or Eagle Hunter.

This photograph taken by Edward Curtis shows a Hopi mother carrying her child on her back.

Hopi children had the run of the village. They played games with their cousins and helped their parents with daily tasks. Children played with marbles, tops, and dolls. Grownups sometimes played games with them, such as a board game called *Totolospi*, a stick and ball game like hockey, tag, and an exciting nighttime hide-and-go-seek game where the person who is "it" sneaks around the other players and loudly bangs a drum.

In the beginning, the Hopi believe, the earth was created by the Sun Father, **Tawa**. The first creatures he brought to life were insects, including his special messenger, Spider Woman. The insects lived in darkness, deep underground. Tawa told Spider Woman that he was going to make a better Second World and asked her to guide the creatures to it. Spider Woman did so, and as the insect creatures climbed up to the new world, they changed. Some grew tails, fingers, or fur. But in the Second World the creatures began to attack and eat each other. Tawa was unhappy. He made a Third World, and again asked Spider Woman for help. This time, she changed the creatures into people. At first, the people were delighted by the beauty of the new world, but soon witches arrived, bringing evil. The people acted greedy and were no

Hopi lands border the Grand Canyon.

longer thankful for their many blessings. Tawa was saddened. Spider Woman gathered a small group of good people and gave them shelter until a better world was found. They sent bird messengers through an opening in the sky to look for a new home. One messenger returned to tell of a world with land, mountains, and rivers. Spider Woman guided the people up a ladder and through the opening into the Fourth World, where the Hopi live today.

When people entered the Fourth World, say the Hopi, invisible spirit beings called **kachinas** were waiting for them. The spirits taught the Hopi how to live in harmony with nature. They taught the Hopi valuable skills such as how to hunt, make tools, plant crops, and heal sickness. The kachinas promised that, if the Hopi showed respect for the gods and took good care of themselves and the earth, the kachinas would deliver rain to grow their food. Then the kachinas left and went to live with the gods on the distant San Francisco Peaks.

Inside a Kiva

In every Hopi village there is a central plaza. In every plaza there is a special underground chamber known as the kiva. Some kivas are small, while others are large and have many rooms. A person enters a kiva by climbing down a ladder. The ladder is a symbol that connects the spirit world below to the human world above. Inside a kiva are altars, fire pits, sand-

Most important ceremonies begin inside a kiva, the center of Hopi religious life.

paintings, and stone carvings that represent important animals and kachina spirits. Each kiva has a small hole, called a *Sipapu*, in the ground that represents the central point from which all life once came. For most of the time this special opening is covered with a stone. During ceremonies, the men stomp on the stone so that the dead who are underground can hear them pray. Except for special events, only men are allowed in kivas. When they gather, the men weave cloth, do wood carving, and plan the year's ceremonies. More importantly, they pray to the spirits for rain, a good hunt, and a bountiful harvest.

Sandpainting

Using colored sand and crushed rock, the Hopi paint on the walls of their kivas. They draw animal spirits and other traditional Hopi designs such as snakes, eagles, corn, clouds, lightning, sun, rain, and rainbows.

To make your own sandpainting you will need:

- Heavy piece of paper or cardboard
- Clear glue
- Wooden tongue depressors or small paintbrushes
- Newspaper
- Colored sand (purchase from craft store or make your own)

To make colored sand you will need:

- 3 cups of sand (the whiter the sand, the richer the color will be)
- Food coloring
- Small plastic sandwich bags
- Rubber or latex gloves

Gather fine sand. Wear gloves when working with the food dye. For each color you use in your painting, put about $1/2$ cup of sand in a sandwich bag and add several drops of food coloring. Close the bag tightly and work the dye into the sand. If you have added too much food coloring, the sand may become too wet. If so, add more sand.

To make your sandpainting:

1· Spread out a folded sheet of newspaper for each color of sand you will be using. You will want to keep the colors separate.

2· Draw your design on the cardboard or heavy paper. Select a color and decide all the areas in the painting where you want that color.

3· Spread glue thinly with a paintbrush or tongue depressor.

4· Take a small handful of sand and let it flow in a slow stream over the areas. You can press it once with the palm of your hand and then shake off the excess sand back onto the newspaper.

5· Select another area and another color and repeat until your painting is finished.

This kachina mask represents the sun and is made of feathers, beads, and animal hide.

Since that time, the Hopi believe the kachinas return for six months every year. The spirits begin to walk toward the Hopi villages in late November. On the first day of winter the Hopi village chief welcomes them with songs and prayers. By February most of the kachinas have arrived to help the Hopi prepare for the growing season. Each clan has its own kachina, such as Eagle, Bear, or Rain Cloud, and during ceremonies, special clan members wear masks and costumes to act as their clan's guiding spirit. Clans are also members of a larger group known as Kachina Societies, which honor the most powerful spirits. When children turn six or seven, they are taught some of the secrets of the Kachina Societies and are accepted as new members.

The Bean Dance Ceremony is the first and most important festival of the kachina season. Celebrations last for sixteen days. Kachina Society members plant bean seeds in the kivas, and when the beans sprout, the human kachina dancers wear masks while they give the plants away. The sprouts make people feel hopeful that their crops will thrive. Public dances are held in the plazas, and the kachinas give carved wooden kachina dolls to the girls and rattles, wands, and bows and arrows to the boys.

Girls are given kachina dolls during the Bean Dance Ceremony.

Hopi Kachinas

Kachinas are special, holy beings in the world of the Hopi. They believe that kachinas are invisible spirits, but in ceremonies, Hopi men portray them. There are more than three hundred different kachinas. They are animals, objects from nature, ancestors, or supernatural beings. Some are clowns. Each kachina has a special role or a message to deliver to the people. Here are some examples:

• White Bear kachinas are very powerful. They are great hunters and healers.

• Kokopelli kachina is very well known. He plays the flute and is either humpbacked or carries a trader's pack on his back. He is a symbol of masculinity.

• Crow Mother is honored by many Hopi as the mother of all the kachinas.

• Ogre Woman kachina teaches manners and good behavior to children. Ogre Woman visits homes and gives each child a few seeds. She tells them that, when she returns, she expects to be fed. If the children do not have food to give her, Ogre Woman tugs at their feet and threatens to eat them.

Each carved kachina doll represents an invisible Hopi spirit.

⬧ Squash kachinas are great runners. During footraces, they dash alongside Hopi racers.

⬧ Koshari kachinas are wildly funny clowns who always wear black-and-white striped costumes and do everything a person should never do. They eat too much, talk too loudly, and say the opposite of what they mean.

⬧ Mudhead kachinas are the most common clown kachinas. They perform in all the dances and often play games with children.

During the colorful displays and parades, clown kachinas dance among the crowds and mock or frighten people into behaving better.

Celebrations continue through spring and summer. Each one is meant to bless the people and their crops. It is also a time for the Hopi to give thanks. In April a planting festival features Hopi footraces. Kachinas urge men and boys to run as fast as they hope the water in the rivers will flow. Once the corn has grown tall, it is time for the kachinas to go home. The last festival, the *Niman*, or "home-going," ceremony begins in early summer. After eight days in kivas, the kachinas

A painting shows three Hopi men performing a traditional dance.

enter the villages at dawn carrying armloads of green corn-stalks and presents for the children. That night the kachinas are thanked by the clans, and the chief makes a speech. Over the next few days the kachinas slowly make their way home to the San Francisco Peaks.

Hopi religion, or the "Hopi Way," gives meaning to daily life. The people believe that all creatures and all things have an inner spirit. The Hopi believe that when people die, their spirits travel down to the underworld. The living pray to their ancestors to send rain. When the men hunt they pray to the spirit of the animal they have killed, to show respect and to thank it for giving up its life. When women make pottery they follow the spirit guiding them in the clay. Since the Fourth World began, the "Hopi Way" has been a rich balance of nature, gods, and the people.

4 · THE FOURTH WORLD TODAY

The Hopi have kept their ancient language, traditions, and crafts throughout the centuries. More than half of the 12,000 present-day Hopi tribal members continue to live on Hopi land.

Today most Hopi people live like other Americans. But they still closely follow the traditions and beliefs of their ancestors. Although Hopi children attend public schools, they are also educated in Hopi language, religion, and customs. Just as their ancestors once did, many Hopi on the reservation continue to work as farmers or craftspeople. After centuries of caring for their crops, Hopi farmers are respected around the world for their ability to grow corn, beans, squash, melons, and wheat on dry land. Traditional crafts made by Hopi **artisans** are featured in museums and collected by

Two boys on Third Mesa overlook the valley surrounding their home.

A Hopi farmer grows corn using special dry-land farming methods.

galleries and art lovers across the nation. On First Mesa, artisans are known for their decorative pottery. On Second Mesa, people make silver jewelry and baskets of coiled grasses and yucca shoots. Artisans on Third Mesa make wicker baskets with colorful patterns. Special woodworkers in the villages carve kachina masks and dolls.

Hopi schoolchildren on a field trip visit a museum displaying Native American art.

The Hopi prefer to live on the land the way the Ancient
Ones did. The people do not have much money, but they
are rich in heritage and in pride. Tourism is an important
way that the Hopi make a living on the reservation. Many
craftspeople sell their pots, baskets, carvings, and jewelry
to visitors. Yet the Hopi keep to themselves. Visitors are not

allowed to view many of the kachina and other special cere-monies and dances that are held in the villages. The Hopi try very hard to protect and preserve their culture.

Hopi religion includes the belief that the land is sacred. The three mesas are entirely surrounded by the Navajo Reservation. The Hopi and Navajo often disagree with one another over land and water rights. But they joined together to protect the San Francisco Peaks, where the Hopi believe the kachinas live. These mountains are not on the reservation. They are more than two hundred miles away, near the city of Flagstaff, and they belong to the U.S. Forest Service. There is a ski resort on the mountains. The resort owners wanted to make snow using water from the city's waste treatment plant. The Hopi and other tribes believed this was an offense to the gods and the holiness of the land. They fought to block the plan, arguing that the San Francisco Peaks were sacred and should not be soiled. There is a law in the United States called the American Indian Religious Freedom Act. It was written to protect Native American religious rites and holy places.

The San Francisco Peaks rise in the distance above a field of wildflowers.

The tribes used this law as a defense in court, but after many years, they lost their case. Yet Hopi leaders did not give up. They fought harder for their cause. Concerned environmentalists joined them. Finally, in March 2007, a federal circuit court ruled in favor of the tribe. The victory brought the Hopi people great relief.

For the Hopi, wherever they live, the three mesas and the San Francisco Peaks are their home in the Fourth World. Every day, for centuries, the Hopi have been careful to tend their ancient land, respect their gods, and faithfully follow the "Hopi Way."

· TIME LINE

Long-term drought forces Ancient Ones to abandon large settlements.

Hopi settle on the three mesas.

The Spanish begin to explore Hopi lands.

Spanish explorer Don Juan Oñate declares that Hopi lands belong to Spain.

Hopi join other tribes and defeat the Spanish in the Pueblo Revolt.

Hopi land becomes part of the United States.

1200s   1500   1540   1598   1680   1848

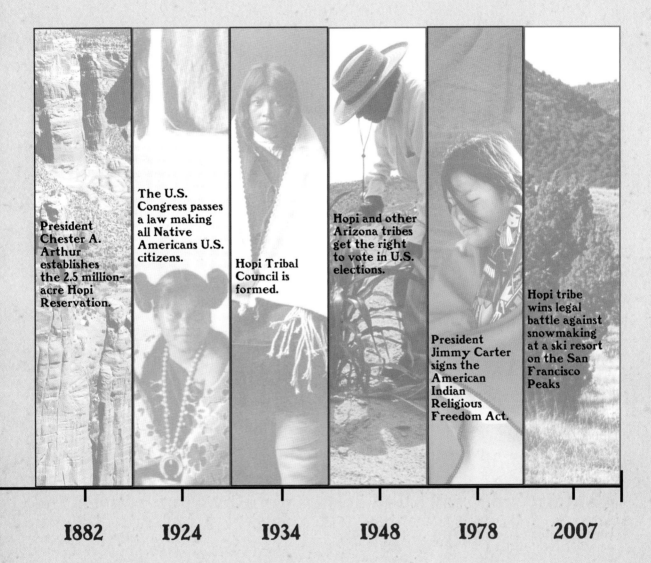

President Chester A. Arthur establishes the 2.5 million-acre Hopi Reservation.

The U.S. Congress passes a law making all Native Americans U.S. citizens.

Hopi Tribal Council is formed.

Hopi and other Arizona tribes get the right to vote in U.S. elections.

President Jimmy Carter signs the American Indian Religious Freedom Act.

Hopi tribe wins legal battle against snowmaking at a ski resort on the San Francisco Peaks

1882   1924   1934   1948   1978   2007

· GLOSSARY

adobe: A building material made of mud and dried into bricks.

artisans: Craftspeople.

box canyons: Dead-end valleys surrounded by steep, rocky walls.

Catholic: Christian faith led by the Pope.

clan: A large family group with a common ancestor.

hostile: Unfriendly, enemy-like.

kachinas: Spirit beings of the Hopi.

kiva: An underground chamber, entered from above by a ladder, where religious ceremonies are held.

mantas: Wide shawl-like dresses worn by Hopi women and woven by Hopi men.

mesa: A wide, flat-topped mountain with steep, rocky sides.

piki: A tortilla-like bread made of cornmeal.

piñon: A pine tree that grows in the desert areas of southwestern United States.

reservation: Land set aside by the U.S. government for Native American tribal use.

sacred: Holy.

sinews: Strong tissues of the body that connect muscle to bone.

Tawa: The Creator, to the Hopi.

Totolospi: A Hopi board game.

turquoise: A blue-colored gemstone found in the American Southwest.

yucca: A cactus, also called _agave_ by the Spanish.

Books

Rosinsky, Natalie M. *Hopi.* Minneapolis, MN: Compass Point Books, 2005.

Ryan, Maria Felkins, and Linda Schmittroth. *Hopi.* San Diego, CA: Blackbirch Press, 2003.

Silas, Anna. *Journey to Hopi Land.* Tucson, AZ: Rio Nuevo Publishers, 2006.

Stout, Mary. *The Hopi.* Milwaukee, WI: Gareth Stevens, 2005.

Web Sites

The Official Hopi Cultural Preservation Office
http://www.nau.edu/~hcpo-p/

Rainmakers from the Gods
http://www.peabody.harvard.edu/katsina/

About the Author

Ruth Bjorklund lives with her husband, two children, and five pets on Bainbridge Island, a ferry ride across Puget Sound from Seattle, Washington. She has written numerous books for young people and enjoys traveling to research her topics. The beautiful and historic American Southwest is a much-loved and cherished destination.

· INDEX

Page numbers in **boldface** are illustrations.